IN A ROOM FULL OF CHAOS, WHERE DO YOU SEE GOD'S HAND?

My Journey Through Separation & Divorce

LATISHA R. RICHMOND

IN A ROOM FULL OF CHAOS, WHERE DO YOU SEE GOD'S HAND?

My Journey Through Separation & Divorce

Copyright @ 2024 Latisha Richmond
ISBN: 979-8-9904970-2-3
All rights reserved.

Author owns complete rights to this book and may be contracted in regards to distribution. Printed in the United States of America.

Library of Congress Cataloging-in-Publication Data

The copyright laws of the United States of America protect this book. No part of this publication may be reproduced or stored in a retrieval system for commercial gain or profit.

No part of this publication may be stored electronically or otherwise transmitted in any form or by any means (electronic, photocopy, recording) without written permission of the author except as provided by USA copyright law.

The Holy Bible, King James Version (KJV). Amplified (AMP) Copyright © 1954, 1958, 1962, 1964, 1965, 1987 by The Lockman Foundation

shero publishing
SHEROPUBLISHING.COM

Editing: SHERO Publishing
Graphics & Cover Design: Greenlight Creations Graphics Designs
glightcreations.com/ glightcreations@gmail.com

IN A ROOM FULL OF CHAOS, WHERE DO YOU SEE GOD'S HAND?

My Journey Through Separation & Divorce

LATISHA RICHMOND

IN A ROOM FULL OF
CHAOS,
WHERE DO YOU SEE
GOD'S HAND?

My Journey Through Separation & Divorce

Table of Contents

Acknowledgements		6
Dedication		7
Introduction		8

Rooms Through My Journey

Room 1	Uncertainty	12
Room 2	Heartbreak	24
Room 3	Doubt	36
Room 4	Sadness	40
Room 5	Confusion	46
Room 6	Loneliness	54
Room 7	Guilt	62
Room 8	Fear	72
Room 9	Firsts	76
Room 10	Recollecting	82
About	Latisha Richmond	90

Acknowledgements

To my Mom and Dad: Thank You for all of the love and support that you have shown the boys and I during this transition. In tough times, it's easy to feel alone, but you've made us feel surrounded by love and strength this entire time. Thank you for standing by me as I had to face a lot in of difficult decisions. You all helped me stand strong with grace and dignity. Thank you both for your guidance, wisdom, and encouragement through this journey. The boys and I are so grateful for everything you've done for us. We love you beyond words.

To my amazing sisters: Tina, Christal, and Princess. You were my first best friends. I know I am technically the "big sister"; however, I admire and look up to you all in more ways than you know. You each have a special place in my heart that nothing else can fill. Thank you for always having my back and being there for me and my boys. I can't put into words how much I appreciate each one of you.

Dedication

For Karter, Kaleb, and Kohen. This book is a testament to our bond that endures, even in the face of our life's challenging chapters. You are my heart and my inspiration. It is a privilege to be your mother. I hope that even through the many transitions we recently weathered together, you know the one thing that always stayed constant was my love for each of you. My goal is to raise you to be young men with character, integrity, and boldness; anchored in the principles from the word of God.

This book is also dedicated to You—whether you've been through a journey like mine, are getting ready for your own journey, or are currently figuring out how to find peace after life's chaos. I hope my story helps you in some way and nudges you to trust in God like never before, no matter what your journey currently looks like.

Introduction

Choosing to step away from what felt like a societal marriage club, something I longed to be a part of since I was young, has been the most challenging decision I've faced to this day. Growing up, marriage always was the ultimate goal for me, and I did achieve it. My marriage survived the anticipated challenges and hurdles. However, when the chaos began to be too much, I saw the need for a change for my boys and me. I decided it was time to walk away. I struggled to embrace my decision; then I realized, the marriage may have failed, but I was not a failure!

Every story has two sides, and in every marriage or relationship, there are distinct perspectives. However, this isn't my "side of the story." It is my journey of how my life's challenges aimed to break me but ultimately played a pivotal role in shaping me into the much stronger woman who exists today.

The book is unique in that it is not only about my journey through separation, and managing life now as a single mother, but it is my real time account that I was able to document during this first year journey of seeing God even through the chaos.

I started writing in my journal and recording voice memos about a year and a half before my journey actually began. Journaling has always been therapeutic for me, but when things started taking a turn for the worst, I knew I needed to write down certain details of specific events. I was being challenged on my account of events, so I started taking notes to keep track of dates, events, and things that happened, even before I made the decision to walk away. Making voice memos allowed me to record my feelings and real and raw emotions in real time.

This is me literally walking you through the chaos I experienced while being separated, adjusting to being a single mom, learning how to co-parent, having a full-time job, helping out at my church, trying to remain strong for my boys and the many emotions of dealing with it all. This is a recap of how I used my challenges to grow, find blessings through the pain, and witness how God used every situation for my good. My hope is that, regardless of your challenges, my book will give you a fresh perspective on your situation, and renewed faith that God is working even in the midst of your chaos. This journey taught me to trust God in ways I never had to before, and for that, I am grateful.

Amidst the turmoil within the walls of what was once called our home, I discovered God's presence in the room. My prayer and hope for you is that, when you find yourself in a room filled with what feels like chaos and uncertainty, after you pause to take a deep breath, you'll also take a moment to look around and seek the hand, the heart or the help of God. I guarantee, in some shape or form, it is there.

My hope is that my journey will open your eyes to the spiritual blessings in the midst of your own chaos and give you a better perspective on everything that you face in life. As you will see from my journey, while things do not always go your way, and the road can be rough, God still has you and He is still there, in the midst of your storms. I believe knowing and being reminded of this will help you to walk with Him, in a different way.

IN A ROOM FULL OF CHAOS, WHERE DO YOU SEE GOD'S HAND?

My Journey Through Separation & Divorce

LATISHA RICHMOND

Fear is not my future,
Hello peace,
Hello joy,
Hello love,
Hello strength,
Hello hope,
It's a new horizon.

"Fear is Not My Future" by *Todd Galberth*

ROOM 1
Uncertainty

Room of *Uncertainty*

"You may now kiss the bride"...

My Godfather declared in a room filled with friends, family, coworkers, and a few curious strangers peeking from around the corner. We stood beachfront, overlooking the ocean on a windy and somewhat rainy Saturday in July. In that moment, we became a married couple, and my life took a new course.

We tied the knot in 2013, bought our first home in 2014, and welcomed our first son a few days after closing. It felt like I was living my own personal romantic comedy. Which are my favorite movies, by the way. I had always had a job in some sort of sales position since college. In 2016, I decided to take Real Estate Pre-Licensing classes. It was something I had wanted to do for a while but had never gotten around to it. Now, I felt like it was time. My plan was to take the classes on my days off, while continuing to work full time in sales, all while being pregnant. I knew it was going to be a lot. However, I had an amazing support system that was willing to help me make it happen.

In my sales job, I normally worked weekends, leaving Tuesdays and Wednesdays as my normal days off. After some research, I discovered a Real Estate pre-licensing class that met only on those specific days. This meant I wouldn't have a day off for eight weeks, all while being pregnant with my second son and having a toddler at home. I was also commuting an hour to work, one way. I had made up in my mind that I was going to do it, and I was determined to make it work!

Real Estate class kicked off, and as usual, I took my seat on the front row, right side—my normally preferred spot in school, church, and seminars. Armed with all the recommended books and materials, I felt ready. However, as the weeks passed, it became clear that I wasn't fully grasping the information under the guidance of my less-than-ideal teacher. My practice tests and homework assignments revealed a gap in my understanding. My grades on the test and practice exams were not where they needed to be.

Determined to turn things around, I decided to take matters into my own hands. I started doing more research and finding other resources to study. Then, I turned to YouTube, hoping to supplement my learning independently. With an hour-long commute each way, I decided to use that time as an opportunity for extra learning instead of the usual calls with my family and friends or blasting my favorite music.

I stumbled upon a YouTube teacher whose style really resonated with me, making the concepts clearer and easier for me to understand. On my way to class, I started listening to his videos that corresponded to our scheduled topic for the day, getting a preview before the actual class. Then, on my way home, I revisited the material again, reinforcing my understanding through repetition. Despite initial discouragement, my hard work paid off- I successfully passed the class!

Now came the time for the State and National Test, which I took shortly after successfully completing the class. Eager to take it while the information was still fresh in my mind, I scheduled the test for a Tuesday. I approached the day feeling prepared and excited, anticipating the achievement of obtaining my license on that day and walking away as a North Carolina Licensed Real Estate Agent.

After completing the test hours later, I anxiously sat in front of the computer screen, awaiting the appearance of the long-awaited test results. Results were in, State Test Results - *FAILED,* National Test Results - *FAILED.* Shock washed over me. On that day, the screen displayed the word **Failed** in bold letters. The room, filled with others awaiting their results, suddenly became a place of heightened emotions. This was the first time that I could recall, in a while, experiencing real failure.

Growing up I made every sports team I had ever tried out for. I was even recruited and asked to play soccer while I was on the basketball court because of my athletic ability. I was hired for every job that I had ever interviewed for. I wasn't used to failure. So, when I saw the word- **Failed** on the screen after I took my first National and State Test it was a new feeling. How could I have failed? Yes, I had failed at something, but I knew I wasn't a failure. In that moment, I made up in my mind that I was going to try again. I had paid money for the class; I had spent a lot of time studying and re-arranging schedules to make the class schedule work. I wasn't going to stop now. But seeing the word *FAILED- hurt.*

As sadness and anger turned into embarrassment, I glanced around to see if anyone else had noticed my screen. I felt overwhelmed, so I quickly gathered my purse, grabbed my water bottle, and exited the room with my head held low. When I got inside my car, I locked my doors, and I couldn't hold it any longer. I dropped my head, grabbed my pregnant belly and tears just began to fall. I was so upset that I had **failed.**

After crying for a few minutes, still sitting in my car, I wiped my eyes and grabbed my notebook from the passenger seat and began writing down everything that I remembered from the test. I wanted to write it down while it was fresh on my mind. After sitting there for almost 20 minutes, writing down everything that came to mind, I drove off and began to call my family to tell them the bad news.

I used the notebook from my car and my other study materials for the next few weeks and then scheduled a time to take the State and National test again. Test Day came and I was there again sitting at the computer waiting for my results. Again, I stared at the screen and waited anxiously for the results. The results were in, State Results: *Failed*, National Results: *Passed*.

I grabbed my stuff and walked with my head down; but not quite as low as before. I went to my car, still cried, but grabbed that notebook again from my passenger seat and began writing down everything I remembered from the State exam.

I used this material again to study and went back to take the exam for my third time. I went in to take only the State exam portion at this point since I had already passed the National Test. Test Day came and results are in, State Exam: *Passed*.

I sat there in awe for a few seconds, just taking it all in and then my baby boy inside my stomach kicked. It was the sweetest nudge. As if he was giving me a high five. I thought to myself in that moment: I am now a Licensed Real Estate Agent in North Carolina. All my hard work had paid off!

In the face of setbacks earlier in the process, I was determined not to brand myself as a failure. Confronted by the word - **Failed** on the computer screen after each attempt, I made a commitment to take thorough notes, capturing what I remembered: useful phrases to study, questions that posed challenges, and topics that had proven to be stumbling blocks. Through tears and frustration, I documented my notes with the intent of revisiting and studying them later, driven by the belief that it was only a matter of time before I would retake the test, hoping for a different outcome, and thankfully that was the case.

Fast forward seven years, and it wasn't a failed test I was dealing with, but a failed marriage. Taking cues from my past, I turned to what I knew. Sitting in my car again, about to walk in to initiate and sign the paperwork to start the separation process, I turned to my phone, this time to do voice memos instead of using a pen and paper. I grabbed my phone, and I began recording as I sat there and talked on my phone and explained every emotion and feeling I was experiencing at that time. Initially it started out as just a therapeutic exercise with a goal of helping me process my thoughts, feelings, and the reality of the situation, but now it evolved into something more. What began as a personal reflection tool is now something that I hope will offer your insight and support as you navigate your own journeys in life. In sharing part of my testimony here, I hope this not only validates your own journey but also offers hope and encouragement if you are facing similar challenges or seeking guidance.

Now, let's get to it. Fast forward about 5 years from the time I became a North Carolina Licensed Real Estate Agent. Work was going great, I was pregnant with my third son, my 2 older boys were getting big and doing so well, but my marriage on the other hand was not. The world felt like it had stopped personally, but professionally things had speeded up. I was just starting to feel like I was getting the grasp of the Real Estate world, at least from the Builders' side that is. Then out of nowhere, *BAM,* the Pandemic hit, and the housing market went insane. I was working for a production home builder; interest rates were low, and the world was now introduced to a new existence- a virtual world. We were able to do more things virtually than we had ever before. It took a lot of getting used to at first. Life as we knew it had changed completely, work was so busy; then my marriage hit rock bottom. Have you ever had so much going on and so much to do, that you just sat and did nothing? Well, that was my reality for months. I felt like I was just going through the motions, and everything was spiraling out of control. But as you know, even when your life is full of *chao*s, the world continues.

In my world, People were buying homes left and right. Some sight unseen and most over asking prices. It was something I had never seen before. I was selling homes faster than I had ever done in the past. Things were going well. Well, from the outside at least it appeared that way. But from the inside it was a completely different story. Homes were selling but they were delayed in closing. The build time, on some of my homes, was going from 8 months to around 18 months. Now, keep in mind, I don't get paid until the homes I sell, close. So, I was going more than double my normal length of time without getting paid my commission. I was my trying my best believe and trust God, but I was stressed.

During our marriage we didn't have a combined written budget. So even though I was on maternity leave, my bills were my bills and I still had to figure out a way to pay them. My budget was extremely tight. I started to consider if I needed to take out a loan or withdraw from my 401K. I tried to withdraw funds, but I wasn't able to.

In this room full of uncertainty, where did I see God's hand? Looking back now and seeing how my 401K has grown substantially over these last few years, I can undoubtedly say, that was actually God's hand protecting my finances. I was denied the opportunity to withdraw the funds; but now I see that was for the better. While I was working things out and making ends meet, my bills continued to pile up and my commissions still hadn't come in yet. Throughout this time, I was still paying my tithes and offerings and being faithful with what I had and believing that God would make a way. I couldn't see how it was going to work out, but I kept believing it would work out.

In July of 2021, during the pandemic, I gave birth to my youngest son, Kohen. During this time, I again was happy on the outside and stressed on the inside. I was blessed to be able to stay home for the maximum amount of time of my maternity leave before having to return to work. When I came back to work, I had a draw style salary that covered me until I could close on my homes that I had already sold. Unfortunately, my base salary was a draw, meaning that I had to pay it back once my homes closed and I got my commission for the sale. So, I was making sales, but the money was not coming in, yet. My draw kept increasing and I was getting more and more in debt to myself. This meant that even when my homes did close later, I had to pay myself back from the previous months, so it would take time until I broke even and even more time to be in the positive.

The pandemic was still in full effect, and it felt like so many people were dying every day. I was able to stay home and sell homes virtually. I believe one of the good things that came out of the new normal we were all forced into, was an overwhelming acceptance of being able to work from home. I was able to arrange virtual appointments to meet with clients daily and was still able to sell multiple homes a month. God was providing for me even through there was so much uncertainty in the world.

Where did I see, God's hand? Even in a pandemic, I was able to deliver my healthy baby boy, and we both left out of the hospital happy and healthy. When my homes did close and after I paid myself back from the draw, I received the biggest commission checks in my career, back-to-back! The way that my homes were closing, it was bringing in solid checks, one right after the other. The commissions were just flowing in; it was almost overwhelming. But in a good way, of course. *Even through the chaos,* God was making a way for us. We had just experienced so much lack, but after just a few months He had turned my entire financial situation around. God was making provisions for me and working all things out for my good!
Romans 8: 28

ROOM 2
Heartbreak

Room of *Heartbreak*

In 2022, I reached a pivotal moment: the decision to end my marriage became clear. It wasn't an impulsive decision by any means, but rather the result of a journey involving prayer, counseling, and deep reflection. For about two years, I wrestled with the idea, constantly talking myself out of it for one reason or another. At first, I thought I should tough it out for my own sake. Then, it was all about my boys—I couldn't bear to put them through it. And let's not forget the pressure of keeping up appearances in my church community and with my family and friends.

But as time passed, the walls of my home felt increasingly suffocating. It was a tough realization to confront, especially considering my upbringing in the church. My parents who have been married for over 30 years were the pastors, and my husband and I always sat on the front row, seemingly the happy and perfect couple. How could I really go through with this?

The burden of expectations weighed so heavy on me. Some people looked up to us and saw us as the couple who had it all together. I felt this weight of responsibility not to disappoint anyone. But you know what? I was completely wrong. I came to realize that I had to prioritize my own well-being. So, I made up my mind—it was time to walk away. *Now, what?*

After I signed the papers there was a lingering pain in my chest from the grief of losing my husband, who was also my best friend. I can't describe it, but it's a pain that feels like an internal ache, a physical heartache that would never go away. It felt like there was something literally sitting on my chest, and it was heavy.

During all the chaos I tried to prepare myself as best as I could. I had no clue where to even begin. Then, one day at work, I found myself opening up to a trusted colleague about my plans to possibly separate and move out. Little did I know, she was going through the same exact thing.

Now, I'm not usually one to spill my personal tea and especially not at work. Yet, in that moment, it just felt right, you know? It was like this gut instinct taking over. I guess you could call it women's intuition. Whatever it was, it turned out that my coworker gave me some pretty good advice. She told me not to rush into leaving just yet. Instead, she suggested I talk to a lawyer first and come up with a game plan before making a move.

She texted me a list of attorneys, and I picked one from there, setting up my first meeting within the week. Luckily, the attorney I chose was super patient, walking me through everything. I only knew a few people that had been through a divorce. I felt lost and didn't know what to do. But talking to my colleague opened doors to resources and information that I never knew I needed to explore prior to just moving out.

Looking back, I'm so glad I didn't just wing it without a plan. It's easy to feel like you've got to keep it all to yourself, especially when you're feeling embarrassed or ashamed. But sometimes, getting advice from someone unexpected can be exactly what you need, exactly when you need it. Now, let me make one thing clear: I wasn't asking my trusted colleague whether I should leave or not. I had already made that call. I just needed some advice on what to do next.

Whether it's deciding to walk away or stick it out, that choice is yours and yours alone. No one else can make it for you.

During my separation, my support system has played a crucial role in helping me feel supported, loved, and heard. I noticed how easily I could get rattled, upset, or frustrated at times. This was a lot. This was something I had never experienced before, and it was hard. But with my parents, sisters, brothers-in-law, and a few close friends by my side, I had the strength to navigate through it all and I still am. Their support, coupled with maintaining a strong prayer life and continually seeking wisdom, guidance, and patience from God, truly carried me through the process thus far.

Once I made the decision to proceed with the divorce and came up with an exit strategy, it was time for our attorneys to start discussing the nitty-gritty details of how everything would be divided. It was a lot to wrap my head around. One moment, it felt like we were planning our future together, and the next, we were locked in disputes over money, TVs, household appliances, and child custody.

We had a house together in Elon, North Carolina, where we'd lived for a decade. I decided to let him keep the house and the boys and I would move out. When I shared this news, it stirred up confusion among some of my family and friends. "You're not staying in the house? You don't want him to leave? ", some asked, puzzled by my decision. But for me, that house held too many negative memories. I was ready to start fresh. If you need to make a decision, such as this one, I suggest you weigh all of your options and make the best decision for you.

Despite the doubts from some close friends, I was firm in my choice to leave. I wanted a new space where my boys and I could create positive memories. This part of the process involved making countless decisions, and I can't stress enough how important it is to pray and seek guidance during such overwhelming times. With so many choices to make, many of them with tight deadlines, it was overwhelming to say the least.

Once I made the decision to move out, I prayed to ask God for wisdom and then I turned to my parents to help me decide on a plan. We started looking at apartments in the area, aiming to find a place I could rent until I found a home of my own. But, let me tell you, the rental market was on fire at that time. Prices were skyrocketing, with rents easily topping $2000 a month.

This presented a big change for me, a big financial commitment. Up until then, he had been handling the mortgage payment and I was handling the boys' daycare and aftercare. Now, with the responsibility of rent falling solely on my shoulders, I had to make room for a completely different budget item with so many uncertainties at the time.

My parents came to my rescue, to say the least. They own multiple rental properties and my mom started sharing details with me about a specific property they were planning to sell to an investor after completing renovations. However, with everything unfolding and the boys and I needing a place to stay, they had an idea. They decided not to sell the property but instead to finish the renovations and let my boys and me move into this newly renovated home. It was an incredible blessing, and we were beyond grateful.

Looking back, when they were planning to sell the home, the renovations were taking longer than expected, largely due to the pandemic. But, once again, it was God's hand of provision over the entire situation, because if the home had been completed as initially planned, it would have already been sold when I needed it most. At the time, all of my parents' other rental properties had tenants, so if it weren't for this unexpected completion delay, we might not have had this amazing opportunity to move into this home.

Despite being delayed three times, the completion of the home coincided perfectly with the month my boys and I needed a new place to stay. It was remarkable how seamlessly everything fell into place. It felt like every detail needed for the transition just started to align effortlessly.

In that moment, I couldn't help but feel like God's hand was guiding every step of the way. Despite the unfortunate circumstances, it was clear that I was moving in the will of God. It was a powerful reminder that even in the midst of challenges, there is a greater plan. *Romans 8:28*

God's hand was clearly at work, protecting me from the burden of paying $2,000 or more in monthly rent plus utilities. With this property he provided for me, I had the unwavering support of my dad every step of the way. Since it was one of my parents' homes, my dad took charge of everything. He fixed any issues that arose, helped us move, built a fence in the backyard to give my boys a peaceful and private space to play, and added a concrete slab and a basketball goal so they could play. He even showed me how to use some of his tools while teaching me basic handy skills for household tasks and things I wanted to assemble around my house. My dad went above and beyond for us. He made sure the trash cans were always out by the curb every Wednesday for pickup on Thursday mornings. It felt like I had both my heavenly Father and my earthly father guiding me through every twist and turn of this journey.

It was nothing short of a divine intervention, a testament to the incredible support and love I had from both above and here on Earth.

Even furnishing my new home felt like a move orchestrated by God. With litigation ongoing, I couldn't rely on my personal funds, so I had to turn to my family and friends for financial support during the transition. What happened next was nothing short of miraculous. Friends and family began sending me thousands of dollars to aid in my journey. Before I knew it, I had over $10,000 at my disposal, covering all my needs for the new home, lawyer fees, and even my decorating plans. The support and love surrounding me by family and friends, served as a reminder that even in the toughest times, blessings can come. It was a testament to God once again providing all of my needs. *Philippians 4:19*

It felt as though God had opened doors and poured out His abundance once I closed the door to a relationship that was no longer serving me. It was a profound moment, as if God was instilling in me the confidence and means to move forward in spite of the heartbreak, confusion, frustration, and doubt.

In that pivotal time, it became clear that God was providing for me and my boys. I took it as powerful confirmation, even before officially moving everything out, that I was going to be okay. God's timing and provision was evident, reassuring me that I was not alone in this journey.

Looking back, when I was going through my season of lack, it was a humbling experience. Going from a comfortable six-figure salary to barely scraping by on bills brought a wave of fear and doubt. I won't pretend I didn't worry because—I did. But amidst the worry, there was also a deep-seated trust that God would see me through.

In hindsight, I realize that sometimes God needs to strip away our pride and personal achievements to reveal what truly needs to be removed from our lives. It was a time of breaking down old patterns and rebuilding a stronger, more independent version of myself as a mother to my boys. Now, I'm starting to understand why that season was necessary—it was a period of growth, preparing me to walk more fully in the purpose and plan God has for my life.

Looking back on everything that unfolded after my separation was finalized, it became clear to me how God was protecting and shielding my boys and me from unforeseen challenges.

Having time to reflect, I thought about something: During the last few years of my marriage, we had been planning to relocate to Raleigh. With me already working there, with friends in the area, and the excitement for a fresh start, the idea seemed promising. We researched various locations in the Raleigh area, toured homes, and was in the process of narrowing down certain areas in Raleigh we were open to exploring for a possible move in the near future.

Given my job was with a Raleigh home builder, we naturally explored the possibility of building our next home with the company I worked for. We visited different communities and settled on the largest floor plan available. We also explored other new communities and checked out homes for sale, weighing our options carefully.

However, you know what? No matter how hard we tried, there were always a few loose ends that needed sorting out before we could make our move to Raleigh. It felt like every time we were on the verge of taking the leap, something would throw a wrench in our plans.

I turned to prayer, asking God to guide us and make a way where it seemed impossible. We were so determined to make this move, but for reasons beyond our understanding, it just never seemed to work out as we had envisioned. In the end, despite our hopes and efforts, we remained in the Burlington, North Carolina area.

It dawned on me recently, if we had gone ahead with our plan to move to Raleigh, I would've been stuck over an hour away from my family, friends, and church community while going through this separation journey. Dealing with all the chaos of this separation already felt like too much to handle. I can't even begin to imagine handling it all from so far away from the support of my family. It was a constant whirlwind of emails, phone calls, negotiations, custody talks, money decisions— you name it, both lawyers were on it. But through all the mess, my family was my rock. Having my parents just a six-minute drive away during that whole process felt like God looking out for me so that I didn't feel alone.

ROOM 3
Doubt

Room of *Doubt*

My First Weekend as a Single Parent

Since it was our first weekend together, just me and my boys, I figured it was time for some fun. We needed it. They'd been going on and on about wanting to visit Great Wolf Lodge, so I figured it was time for us to go. So, I went all out planning this trip. It was our first solo adventure, and I was determined to try not to forget a single thing, so I spent more time than usual packing up all our gear.

When we finally pulled up to the Lodge, I parked in the front temporary parking spot. And man, it hit me like a ton of bricks. There I was, all alone, with a car packed to the brim with luggage and three rowdy boys – ages 8, 6, and 1 – and to top it off, it was pouring down raining. I couldn't help it; tears just began to fall down my face. But I quickly pulled myself together and wiped my face before my boys could notice.

Got the car unpacked, checked in, then had to deal with parking and getting all the boys out in the pouring rain. After that, it was a juggling act of hauling luggage while the boys were demanding snacks, bombarding me with questions, and trying to explore on their own. And oh yeah, I was also pushing a stroller and a luggage cart at the same time. It was a lot.

It was my first-time handling all three boys on a solo trip. But once I finally got everyone settled into the room, let me tell you, it felt like a huge win! I might've even done a little victory dance by myself in the bathroom in celebration.

I got them each the VIP Experience pass, and boy was it worth it. They were able to do all the activities and seeing them with the biggest smiles on their faces for two days straight was like a breath of fresh air. It was so good for us to break out of our regular routine and just relax together. Sure, there were times when it hit me that this was the start of me going on trips as the solo parent and figuring details out on my own. But you know what? Despite the bumps along the way, this first adventure was totally worth it. Seeing my boys' smiles and hearing their laughs, as they explored the entire lodge and were just so happy, made all the hard work pay off.

When we returned, I took time to pray and felt peace about posting to social media and announcing our separation. May not seem like a big deal to some but for me it was a big ordeal. My reason for this was because over the past 10 years I had always posted all of the good things that had happened in our relationship. I felt it was only right to tell the other side of the story. Once I hit post, I felt so relieved. I felt free! A few hours after I posted it, I was surprised to see all of the likes, comments, and private messages. At certain times, if you have a peace about it, it is good to be transparent about your situation, especially when facing a separation or divorce.

ROOM 4
Sadness

Room of *Sadness*

I had the boys for the first few days after our separation was final. Now it was time for them to go be with their dad for a few days. I found myself breaking down. I was driving and it hit me like a ton of bricks, that the boys were with their father tonight. I realized that I didn't have to rush home as I typically did while my husband and I were together. I didn't have to worry about cooking the boys' dinner tonight, helping them with their homework, or getting them situated with baths and lunches. It hurt.

I felt this overwhelming sense of not being needed anymore. But that wasn't true. My boys did need me. They just were being cared for by their father at the moment. The enemy tried to put all kinds of negative thoughts and ideas in my head, and I had to combat that with the word of God. I was needed. My boys would always need me; I am their mom. They needed me praying for them daily when I had them or when I didn't. They needed me to be emotionally healthy for myself and for them. They just needed me differently right now. And that was perfectly okay.

When I came home, I fixed some shrimp tacos. One of my favorite meals. I decided to curl up on the sofa and watch a movie, but it was so quiet. The quiet was hard. I had broken down today, but I was okay. I made it through. *Celebrate the small wins.*

The next day, Karter had a baseball game. After the game, the boys would go with their dad. But at least I would get to see them. Karter did great in his game. This would be my first time seeing them out and about, but not being able to bring them home. Things did, however, get a bit tense afterwards. I had Kohen with me during the game. So afterwards, we were walking to the car and my ex tried to grab him from my arms kind of aggressively. I ignored him. I had prepared some special treats to give them after their game. I went to my car to get them, and my ex got a little pushy and impatient. I tried to stay strong for the boys, but as soon as I was alone in my car, the emotions hit me, and I couldn't hold back the tears.

That night, I had to swing back to our old place to pick up my other car and some items. When I got there, the boys started asking if I'd hang around for dinner. Then, out of the blue, my ex offered up pizza and wings. Karter, overhearing, got all excited and insisted I stay. So, despite feeling a bit awkward, I ended up joining them for dinner. It felt weird. But again, at least I got to see my boys and spend more time with them.

Then, my ex surprised me by asking if I'd put Kohen to bed. I paused for a moment. Yeah, it would've made things easier for him since I usually handled bedtime. But honestly, I didn't really care about that. What mattered most was spending time with my son. So, I went ahead and rocked Kohen to sleep. And you know what? He was out like a light in just 15 minutes.

As I was getting ready to leave, I wanted to say goodnight and goodbye to my two older boys. Karter, being his usual self, asked for a bedtime story. It was their classic go-to-move. Whenever bedtime rolled around, they'd suddenly need another story, more kisses, or want to share every detail of their day. So, I started making up a story for them.

But then, in walks my ex, rushing me to wrap it up and get the boys to bed. I told him to " give me 5 minutes." In that moment, I saw a glimpse of the old him resurface. He'd be nice when it suited him, but the minute that was over, he acted and treated me differently. It was a very subtle, yet harsh reminder that I was making the right call by moving on.

With that realization, a wave of freedom washed over me. It was confirmation; I didn't have to stay in the chaos, like I had for the past decade. I had the power to walk away. And as I made my exit, my ex stopped me with a request: "Hey, the 25th is my Thursday, but could you take the boys?" I knew he was waiting for me to ask why or what he had going on, but I didn't inquire. Instead, I simply said, "Sure." It felt empowering to not care what he did with his time away from the boys and me. For the past few years, I had stressed about that so much. And that day was the first day that I started to release the desire to know what he was doing and the desire to control it. It was the beginning of a different emotion. *Freedom.*

When I got home, my sister Christal was there with me. It felt amazing not to be alone. We stayed up late, watched movies, and indulged in Reese's cups in bed. Having my sister by my side made all the difference. She truly turned my first night without the boys into a success. I was grateful beyond words for her presence. I wasn't alone, and that was everything.

ROOM 5
Confusion

Room of *Confusion*

Life is a constant series of trade-offs. From the monumental decisions to the mundane ones, we're always weighing our options and making choices. Whether it's the big decisions that shape our futures or the small ones that influence our daily routines, trade-offs are an inevitable part of our journey. Each decision carries its own set of consequences and benefits, shaping the path we ultimately take.

Think about when you decided on your spouse, your job, your car, your house, or your wardrobe. These decisions usually require a tradeoff. Think about the decision regarding your home. I guarantee it involved trade-offs. Choosing the house with the larger lot and superior upgrades might mean exceeding your intended budget. On the other hand, by choosing a home with less space and features, you gain the ideal purchase price, easily manageable within your budget. It's the same when selecting a spouse; at some point, you weighed the positives and negatives and concluded that the positives outweighed the negatives. Or maybe they didn't, but you traded off either way you look at it. If you're trying to decide on Target vs. Walmart, you are mentally weighing the tradeoffs. Chick-fil-A or McDonalds, you are weighing tradeoffs. Often, these decisions are made unconsciously, but whether we realize it or not, we're making trade-off decisions every single day.

Now, finding positivity amidst *chaos* felt nearly impossible. When we agreed to split custody 50/50, there were numerous options presented to us by our lawyers for the weekly breakdown. Ultimately, we settled on a 2-2-3 schedule. This meant alternating custody every 2-3 days and every other weekend. Transitioning from seeing my boys every day to just 3-4 days a week has been an immense adjustment. The first few weeks were filled with tears; and even now, I still have moments that bring me to heartache.

One of the major challenges I faced in adjusting to shared custody was having to walk away from my boys at sports events or school functions on days when it wasn't my *turn* to have them. Saying goodbye to them in those moments was, and still is incredibly difficult. However, the trade-off was that on the days when they weren't with me, I had the opportunity to see them when it wasn't scheduled. *That was a tradeoff.*

Although it was tough to leave them behind on those occasions, there was a silver lining in being able to spend time with them on unexpected days. It required mental preparation to handle those situations, but seeing my boys outside of our scheduled time together was undeniably a positive aspect of the arrangement. It's all about finding the balance and focusing on the moments of connection, even when they occur unexpectedly.

Now, I am in the process of growing to appreciate those nights when I return home alone. They provide me with precious time to decompress, tidy up my home, catch up on laundry, enjoy meals without interruptions, go to bed early, exercise, or simply enjoy moments of quiet time. These are things I rarely had during my marriage—a silver lining amidst the *chaos. Another tradeoff.*

I am also growing in the appreciation of knowing that my boys are now benefiting from a healthy balance of time with each one of us separately. It's reassuring to see them adjusting well in our custody arrangement and It's a blessing to be able to provide them with that sense of continuity and stability in the midst of so much change.

When I focus on the positive tradeoffs, it allows me to cope with my new reality. Yes, it is still painful; and yes, I do shed tears, alone, in my car and out of view. However, I pray and push past the grief; to move forward, always trying to find *the good even in the midst of the chaos.*

Being the go-to strong friend and sister has its downsides, especially when I started this process. Something that role felt so much bigger than me. I suddenly didn't feel strong anymore. As the oldest sibling and a leader at work, it's tough to admit when you need help. My family and my boys rely on me. My family calls me *Martha Stewart* since I was always planning and organizing everything, from holidays, to parties and family events. So, when I decided to split from my ex, I told him he could keep the house. But now, here I am, getting used to life in a smaller place and not being the event planner and leader of everything like I used to be. It's a shift, for sure, but my family has been quick to adapt. They've embraced this new version of me, flaws and all, and their support has been a real lifeline as I figured things out.

However, my smaller space is so peaceful, and calming; and it's only full of good memories. Memories of me starting fresh. Memories of my dad and I moving new furniture in each room. Memories of my friend and I designing the boys' room and seeing their faces as they walked in seeing all new items.

Memories of late night and early morning dance parties in the kitchen, and mommy and sons' popcorn movie nights, and staying up. *Another Tradeoff.*

There are days when I miss my old life. I sometimes just drive and think and ask myself if I would ever go back. But then I think about how much pain I was in, and how I literally felt like I was suffocating while I was there. I think about my boys and how I miss waking them up every day. I think about the good memories, but the bad ones outweigh the good ones. *Tradeoffs.*

It's dawned on me that I can't always play the role of the tough friend. Those friends who expect me to be the strong one might not be able to handle supporting me through something like a divorce. I'm grateful for the friends and family who can adapt to different roles. So, in this phase of my life, I'm incredibly thankful that God is showing me the importance of trade-offs. Understanding that most big decisions involve giving up something to gain something else is a profound lesson to grasp. It's not a compromise, just a tradeoff.

The concept of trade-offs becomes especially poignant when considering the decision between staying in a marriage or opting for divorce. On one hand, staying in a marriage might mean sacrificing personal freedom or enduring difficult times for the sake of commitment and family unity. On the other hand, choosing divorce could entail giving up the comfort and familiarity of a long-term relationship in exchange for potential personal growth, freedom, and the opportunity to pursue happiness on one's own terms. Both options involve significant trade-offs in terms of emotional, financial, and practical implications. It's a complex decision that requires careful consideration of what one values most and what sacrifices they are willing to make for their own well-being and fulfillment. *I chose to make this tradeoff.*

ROOM 6
Loneliness

Room of *Loneliness*

It seems like I'm wrestling with loneliness more often these days. In just a couple of weeks after we signed the separation agreement, we would have celebrated our ten-year anniversary. For the past almost decade, my life revolved around him and our children. We dated for two years, then had a year-long engagement, so it's been over thirteen years since I've truly been on my own. I've been feeling God nudging me about this. I've made up my mind not to go back, not to reconcile, but loneliness has this way of making you desperate to fill the void.

In this season, I'm learning that what feels like loneliness isn't necessarily that. Sometimes, separation is just God's way of preparing us for something new, something different. Things might be different now, but I'm realizing I'm not truly alone. God's hand is still guiding me, reminding me that He's in control. He's showing me that He's present in all of this and for that I am thankful.

Giving it to God

Kohen's second birthday was fast approaching, and as I typically do for all my sons' birthdays, I was gearing up to make a post. But then, I heard God whispering to me, "*Give me that post.*" He asked me, "If you give me that post and don't share, won't he still turn two?" I answered and said yes and did not make my annual post that I was excited about.

I understood what God was telling me, but it was a real struggle. I really wanted to share my son's milestone with the world. Yet, I knew I had to listen and be obedient to the Holy Spirit. So, I made the decision not to post anything and to step away from all social networks for at least 30 days. To some, that might seem like a small thing, but for me, it was a big step at the time. I feel like God was just testing me at the time and I am pretty sure I passed.

During this season of solitude, I am striving to find contentment and learn from what God is doing and teaching me. Already, I've noticed myself growing stronger and more empowered as I trust in Him and strive to walk in His ways, even in the small moments. It feels like God is truly at work within me.

Stepping away from social media has indeed been eye-opening. It has made me realize how much time I was wasting on those platforms and how it was affecting my mental well-being. By cutting out those distractions, I've had more time for myself and for my boys. I sense that God is imparting numerous lessons to me during this time, and I'm doing my best to embrace them.

I made the decision to create a vision board—a tangible way to continue healing from my past relationship while also setting my sights on the future. One thing I wholeheartedly believe, though it may seem premature to some, is that I will find love again. I cherished being a wife, but my time with him had reached its end. I have no doubt that I made the right choice, and I'm eagerly anticipating how God will bless me and have His hand on me during my next season.

I'm walking by faith and trusting that God will provide me with a loving husband in the future. I believe wholeheartedly that this season of loneliness is only temporary, and I'm holding onto that promise as I move forward.

Looking back, When I went back to the house for the first time after moving into my new place, I had my own exit strategy when things got awkward. That brought me an incredible sense of freedom. While I was at the house, sharing dinner and tucking the boys in, I knew deep down that I could leave his space whenever I needed to. It was a stark contrast to times before our separation when I felt trapped within those four walls. But now, that wasn't my reality anymore. I have my sanctuary, my own space to retreat to—a new home just for my boys and me. It feels like freedom, like God's hand is still guiding me, providing for me, and making provisions to ensure our well-being.

During this season, God was really working on me, teaching me the importance of letting go and trusting Him with everything. In the midst of a divorce, you quickly realize how little control you actually have over things. I am learning to surrender and trust God in ways I never have before.

I am learning and coming to terms with the fact that I cannot control my ex's decisions or what goes on in his household. The only thing I can control is how I respond to those decisions and what goes on in my household. I cannot allow his actions or the way I feel or respond to push me out of alignment with who I am and what God wants for my life.

Prayer really does change things. For the aspects of life that are beyond my sight and control, I pray a simple prater during those times: "God, help me see what I can see, but also give me the faith to trust you in the areas where I lack clarity. Give me strength to release my desire to control things that are out of my control because I know you are always in control." I'm learning to rely on God to handle the things I can't control, trusting that He's working everything out according to His plan for my boys and me. I'm trusting Him to lead my boys and me toward what's best for us.

I've come to understand that God loves my boys even more than I do. Which has to be a whole lot. Realizing this, I didn't want my attempts to control certain situations to limit the blessings He had in store for us. So, I surrendered to His will, asking Him to fulfill my requests—or even better, since He alone knows our future and what's truly best for us, for His will to be done. And with that, my prayers began to change...

"God, you know the desires of my heart. I know that you said in your Word that you can do exceedingly and above what I ask or think. So, I ask for your help through this <u>separation</u>. This is a way I have never traveled before, and I need your wisdom and guidance every step of the way. I trust you with my boys and I trust you to watch over them when I am with them and when I am not. There is a lot that is now no longer in my control, and I need your help to release those things to you. Please continue to do a work in me."

I encourage you to trust God in whatever situation you are currently dealing with. If it is not a separation or a divorce, replace a few words from my prayer and make it your own. This simple prayer has been a game changer for me during this season.

Recognizing a shift in my focus, I made the choice to step back from social media once more, aiming to reduce distractions during this period of trusting in God. I've found that sometimes, blocking out certain distractions can lead to clarity in various aspects of life.

I made a conscious decision to limit my interactions to those who truly cared and supported me; scaling back my accessibility to those who didn't fit that category. I started to guard what I shared: from my pictures to my posts and becoming more discerning about who I let into my inner circle. This shift in perspective, guided by God, allowed me to be more intentional with my actions. It also allowed me to reclaim a sense of control over my life while also surrendering more areas to His guidance and direction.

ROOM 7
Guilt

Room of *Guilt*

I have had so much fun with my boys these past few days over the Holiday break. But now, it was time for them to get back to school. I packed up their book bags, dropped them off at school, and prepared not to see them for a few days. This is the part I didn't prepare for. This is the part I couldn't have prepared for.

It's interesting how the structured days and schedules can sometimes create a sense of clock-watching when they're with me. It's as if I find myself counting down the minutes until they depart once again.

But you know what? I've decided to change that up a bit and start thinking of it differently. Instead of focusing on my time with them slipping away, I'm choosing to see our time together as time to make memories and try new things. I've started being more intentional with our moments, soaking up every bit of laughter and love we can squeeze in. Because in the end, it's those moments that really count and the ones we will look back on and truly remember.

Breaking up is hard. Sharing custody is hard. Dealing with guilt is hard. I was so accustomed to having my boys by my side every single day, and now I have to split my time, schedule mommy-sons outings, and prepare myself for the moments when I'm on my own. I feel so guilty that this is now my reality.

I'm still adjusting to this whole shared custody thing. Just when I think I've got the hang of the schedule and routine, something throws me back to square one. But you know what? I'm learning to give myself grace. I'm giving myself permission to feel all the emotions, whatever those may be. I am learning it's all a part of the process.

I have had to rely on God so much during this process. During the many moments where I feel weak and sad that, I call on him to be my peace. *Philippians 4:7.*

If I can be completely honest, I don't understand this. I do not understand why this is now my reality. I got married to be married and to stay married. However, things don't always work out like we have planned and that is okay. I am trusting God through this, even though I don't understand. I know God is still in control, and even though I do not know the plan, I believe it is working out, and that he is able to do exceedingly above all that we ask or think. *Ephesians 3:20*

During this entire transition, there's been a lot of stuff completely out of my hands. It's been a real adjustment for me. But you know what? Instead of stressing about what I can't change, I'm putting my energy into what I can control. *One big thing.* Making sure I'm there for my boys. I've started these little "check-ins" with them every few days, just to see how they're really doing with all the changes. Recognizing the weight of the situation on both them and me, I've come to appreciate the importance of providing them with the space to express their feelings in the midst of all of the chaos.

I started with my oldest, Karter. I wanted to check in and see how he was doing, how he was feeling. And you know what he said? He was excited about having two Christmases soon, two sets of gifts. That would be the first thing he says, right. But then he got real with me. He said he didn't like not seeing me every day. That hit me hard. I knew I had to do something, make sure he felt connected to me, even if we were apart physically. So, I got my oldest boys Gizmo watches. These little things let us FaceTime whenever they wanted. Suddenly, they could reach out to me whenever they needed to.

Next up was Kaleb. He just talked about how he wanted us all back together again like before, and in the same home. It broke my heart to tell him that we couldn't live together anymore. We had a good cry together and hugged it out. Those moments are tough, but they're necessary. We've had quite a few of them since the separation, but it feels like we're getting better at handling them each time. And for that, I'm grateful.

Kohen was too young to be able to really understand what was going on, but he did understand when I had to leave him during times we would normally be together. He didn't understand, at first, but now he comprehends those talks more and more and I believe it's helped him through this transition.

The Other Side

In motherhood, especially now as a single mom, exhaustion is just part of the package! Before my separation, juggling work, laundry, cleaning, and all the mommy duties left me drained most of the time. But you know what? One silver lining to this separation is that I now get these little breaks. They're like pockets of time just for me, what I like to call "Tish time." Not mommy time. Not work time. Just Tish time. It's been eye-opening, realizing that there's more to me than just being a mom. I'm exploring new interests, figuring out where I want to go, what I want to eat — it's liberating!

These breaks also give me a chance to catch up on all the household chores, like cleaning, laundry, and getting organized. And speaking of organization, I had this idea to get a chore chart for the boys. I purchased one from Amazon and I listed out all their daily chores, and let me tell you, it's been a game changer. Not only has it given the boys more accountability and responsibility, but it's also smoothed out our morning and evening routines.

Now, thanks to the chore chart, the boys have the tools they need to handle their responsibilities without me hovering over them every morning. They mark off each chore with a star once it's done, and let me tell you, it's made a world of difference. This morning was a prime example. We actually managed to leave the house without any yelling or meltdowns — it actually was efficient and peaceful. And as if that wasn't enough of a win, we even got out of the house a little earlier than usual. Talk about a victory!

But wait, there's more! I've decided to add a little extra incentive with a treasure box to reward their new routines and added chores. So, at the end of each week, the boys can earn rewards for their hard work. It's like a little added motivation to keep them on track, and so far, it's working like a charm. In addition to the chore chart and treasure box I have also been more intentional about us spending more time reading the bible together.

Through all recent twists and turns, there are a few things I aim to keep steady for them. That's God's love, my love, and teaching them to love themselves. I'm convinced that if these stay constant and they keep building a solid relationship with Jesus, they'll be just fine even through the chaos.

I also started these morning *Encouragement Lines,* with my boys. Right before we walk out of the door for school, I tell them to line up and they form a line. Now of course they always go back and forth about who is first, second, and third. But outside of that, I take about 15-20 seconds, with each of my sons, to pour into them. I get down to their eye level and hold both of their hands and pour into them.

Karter... Are you ready to have a great day? Let's be great today!
Karter... You are so intelligent.
You are an amazing friend.
You are an awesome big brother.
You are an incredible son.
You have the best jokes.
You are so kind.
You are so funny.
You are a leader and not a follower.
You listen to the voice of the good shepherd and the voice of the stranger you will not follow.
You are enough!
And Mommy loves you, your family loves you, and God love you!

I repeat the *Encouragement Lines* with each of my sons daily. I don't care if I'm running a bit late; I always make time. It literally only takes a minute of our morning, but it's such valuable time. It is a regular part of our morning routine when they're with me. Every time I take those 60 seconds of encouragement, my sons' faces light up. My youngest always says, "Again, Mommy! Let's do it again!" I am affirming to them every day that they are with me.

One thing that I do for me, is that I've found it helpful to make audio journal entries, on my phone, during my long commute to work. It's a private way to reflect and document my thoughts and feelings. I've also made it a habit to treat myself to some form of self-care every month. Whether it's a spa retreat, therapy session with a licensed therapist, indulging in a meal at a new restaurant (even if I'm dining alone), going to a bookstore and buying myself a few books, buying myself fresh flowers, trying out a new hobby, or revisiting an old one, just to name a few. It's important to prioritize my well-being especially during this transition.

Despite the challenges of this transition, I've discovered that I have to try seeing the good and making good use of the time apart from my boys. I am learning to try to embrace our time apart instead of dreading it. I know now that it is an inevitable part of this process. If I learn how to embrace it, I know that it will help me get through it. It has been giving me a chance to recharge and pour it into my own cup. So that when my boys return, I can fully focus on them.

I've also created a special space in my room that has my vision board, prayer requests, and encouraging quotes, a desk, a comfy chair, a cute lamp, and my favorite blanket. It's a sanctuary just for me, off-limits to my boys. It has been so instrumental and therapeutic for me spending time there. If you can create a space just for you in your home, do it. If you needed a sign to do so, this is it. It's been life changing for me, and I hope the same for you. I'm grateful for the Holy Spirit's guidance in these new practices, which allow me to show love and honor to Him while being intentional in loving and caring for my boys and myself.

ROOM 8
Fear

Room of *Fear*

Growing up in church all my life, hearing prophetic words is something that I have grown accustomed to. When a Pastor, First Lady, or Missionary comes to minister at church they sometimes flow in the ministry of prophetic anointing. This allows God to minister and speak to other people through them. Sometimes the word or prophecy is for you, and they come and tell you directly and sometimes it's a general word.

Yesterday, I attended my childhood church, Evangel Fellowship's Women in Ministry-WIM Conference. During that conference, the speaker, Barbara Bryant, was truly amazing. She spoke on the topic; *I am a Mustard Seed*. She spoke about faith and the things that are birthing inside of us that need to be watered, grow and bear fruit. She shared that we each have mustard seeds inside of us and that we don't need to be afraid, but rather, step out on faith to do the things that God is calling us to do.

During her speech, she repeatedly emphasized the phrase "FINISH THE BOOK!" It resonated deeply with me because it echoed a sentiment I had been struggling with - the need to complete my own book, this very book. It felt as though her words were tailor-made for my ears. The desire to bring my story to fruition had been burning within me, and her relentless encouragement ignited a newfound determination. Through audio recordings, I've been documenting my journey, believing that I'm being guided by a higher purpose to inspire and uplift others. Hearing her impassioned plea to "Finish the Book" sparked a renewed sense of purpose within me, moving me forward with an unwavering resolve.

After the service, the speaker came directly to me and laid hands on me. She spoke entrepreneurship over me. She kept saying, "I see entrepreneurship on you." As she touched my stomach and my head repeatedly, she said, *"Entrepreneurship, Entrepreneurship, don't worry about the resources. You've got a mustard seed growing in the inside of you. And God said, all you have to do is go forth and he's going to bring it to pass."*

I was really on the fence about going to church that day. I mean, I was stressed out to the max and just had this huge blow-up with my ex over a custody disagreement. But despite all that drama, I decided to go to church anyway, and man, am I glad I did! Sometimes, when there's a word from God waiting for you at a service, meeting, or even just hanging out with a friend, it seems like the enemy throws everything it's got to mess with your head and make you think staying home is a better idea. But here's the thing: when you notice that happening, take it as a sign to push through anyway. Trust me, there's usually something good waiting on the other side of all that chaos. The enemy's whole deal is to mess with your head and stop you from getting where you need to go. But don't let that stop you. Even if you're crying your eyes out or feeling like your heart's been stomped on, just keep pushing forward. I've lost count of how many times I've shown up to church or meetings right after some big fight or a good old cry. And you know what? Every time, I'm so glad I went anyway.

This journey can be hard, let me correct that, this journey *will* be hard. It will take a lot out of you. However, let God re-fill your cup and what you have lost. He will fill you up and restore you. *Seek ye first the kingdom and his righteousness, and all these things will be given to you. Matthew 6:33*

ROOM 9
Firsts

Room of *Firsts*

This past year has been hard, there is no doubt about it. But you know what? I've got this feeling deep down that it's all leading up to something incredible. I'm excited to see what God has planned.

As I keep rolling with the — what feels like punches, I'm thinking about how my entire life has changed drastically over these last few months. This whole journey has really changed me in ways I never would have imagined.

But you know what the best part is? I do, however, feel stronger and more faithful to God than I ever have before! Despite all the struggles, my boys and I are adjusting well. Watching us grow closer together, watching them lean on one another more, and watching them grow closer to God and develop a heart for things of God has truly been a blessing. They've got these sincere hearts for Him, and I pray every day that God keeps leading them and me closer to him.

Kaleb, he's got this genuine love for God that just shines through. He loves worship music and loves to walk around the house while singing whatever worship song is on his heart. He loves to have quiet prayer and bible time before bed. I pray that God keeps leading him down the right path.

Now, Karter, he's a natural-born leader, just like me. Always looking out for everyone and trying to make sure everyone is okay. He takes time to study the word and pray in private. He often gets shy if asked to pray in public but doesn't hesitate to pray with us in private. I pray that God continues to work in him and make him a leader for His glory.

And then there's my little Kohen, who's such a mama's boy. I call him my worshipper. He loves to pray every morning and he loves quoting the scriptures he has memorized. I pray that God keeps shaping him into the man He wants him to be.

For all three of my boys, I pray that God uses them for His purpose, strengthening them and granting them a peace that's beyond understanding. I ask for strength, power, and guidance for them, and for myself as their mother.

Throughout this journey, I have realized that sometimes the process can be one of the best parts. I am enjoying this process and taking it one day at a time. I am walking in gratitude.

I encourage you to start writing in a journal or do audio memos, like I did. However, start documenting your journey in whatever method feels comfortable to you. Do this, so that when God does start bringing you out of whatever situation you're dealing with -*Because we all have something* - and answering your prayers you can reflect on a time when you needed God and he answered. This serves as a reminder during the times when you need God. You can reflect on a prayer or situation you struggled with in the past and go to that same place and see how he answered that prayer or brought you out of that situation.

This year was my first Christmas as a Single Mom. It was different and had its tough moments, but we figured out three things that made it a bit easier for us to cope with such a big change.

Created New Traditions

We created new traditions, making fresh memories in new places. Trying out new stuff during the holidays. We went on the Polar Express and we stayed overnight in a nearby hotel. We settled in the hotel first then headed out for the last polar express train ride of the night. They got to eat junk food and stay up "extra late." I signed us up for the VIP experience so we could have seats at our own table. Since I was doing this alone, it would allow them to all be settled and seated for the entire ride! They were excited to see Santa, receive goody bags, and take pictures; they even got to pick out a few treats from the gift shop.

Revisited Old Places

We revisited some old places as well. This gave my boys a sense of familiarity. Bringing along new friends made it even more special. We visited the Mclaurin Farm. It continues to be one of our favorites during the Holiday Season. Since we split custody on Christmas Day- we started our Christmas festivities a day early. So, they woke up early and got to open presents on Christmas Eve AND Christmas Day.

Had Clear Family Communication

I kept my family in the loop about the days and times I had my boys. We also started celebrating early. It's important to celebrate the Holidays during the time you have them. Even if it's a few days late or a few days early. My boys really enjoyed having a longer Christmas Celebration! It helped us make the most of our time together. I'm thankful for my incredible support system! My family moved our annual Christmas Day brunch to Christmas Eve, so we truly had two days of Christmas. It was amazing!

I also proactively communicated with my family about the times and dates I had my boys, and they were happy to switch things up a bit, allowing us to truly maximize on the time we had. A solid support system can truly make all the difference. My family along with my Faith has truly been my rock and my strong foundation in the midst of all this chaos.

Bonus Tip: Plan something fun right after Holiday drop-off so you have something to look forward to. My sister planned a Color Purple family movie outing. It was a lot of fun and the movie was great!

I still teared-up a bit after drop-off and that's okay. But hearing both Kaleb and Karter say, "This was the BEST Christmas Everrrrrr!" right before drop-off made it all worth it!

Don't forget your past but embrace your future.

ROOM 10
Recollecting

Room of *Recollecting*

As my boys, Karter, Kaleb, Kohen, and I embark on this journey that now includes just me and them, I reflect on what could have been, but have more faith in what is to come. This journey will be different; it will have adjustments, pain at times, some tears, but I believe it will mostly include happiness and hope. I'm happy that I have three amazing boys to be on this journey with me, and a great hope for what's to come.

What will this look like? I'm not sure yet, but I know it will include some new firsts, some bitter and some sweet, and that's okay. If you're a believer, please keep my boys and I in your prayers. If you are going through a similar journey or even something completely different, I would also love to pray for you. Feel free to reach out to me so that we can pray for each other.

I've been so fortunate to have an incredible family and support system by my side throughout this journey. My family and my relationship with God have been my firm foundation, and I can't express my gratitude enough. To my support system, you know who you are - thank you. While I may feel uncertain about this unfamiliar path that I find myself on, I take comfort in the knowledge that God has never let me down before, and I trust that He won't start now.

First Year Takeaways

1. Only focus on the things you can control. If it is out of your control, release it and pray about it.

2. If you are splitting custody, consider the sports and activities in which your children may participate. The fact that my boys play a lot of sports was overwhelming to handle at first. It was difficult trying to juggle everything between both of our schedules. However, the boys being in sports allowed me to see them on days that I wasn't "scheduled" to see them. I loved this extra time with my boys, and really noticed how much it helped during this first year of transition.

3. Talk to your children about their feelings and about yours. Believe it or not, having a vulnerable moment with your children can be therapeutic for them and for you.

4. During phone calls and check-ins when your children are with your co-parent, find, figure out and discover new questions to ask them during phone calls. This encourages a more in-depth conversation and breeds connection.

5. Set boundaries and stick to them.

6. Try your best to embrace new things. It will be hard, but it's necessary.

7. Celebrate Anyway: If you have your children around a specific holiday and not on the actual Holiday, it's okay. Celebrate anyway. The specific date doesn't matter as much as the actual memories. Memories matter more.

8. Make the Meal: On days when you are alone and don't have your kids, still cook yourself dinner. Cook yourself a nice meal and sit down and enjoy it. You deserve a nice meal too, even if you're alone.

9. Celebrate your separation or divorce milestones in whatever way makes you happy.

10. Be Present with your children. An extra 10 minutes a day for one year is equivalent to two and half days. Being present can be in-person or on the phone/facetime. Just make it a conscious effort to be present.

11. If your schedule and funds allow- plan spontaneous trips. Pick your kids up with the car packed, and just Go! Thank me later.

12. Take pictures. Capture the memories before it's too late.

13. Take a solo trip. Get a massage. Treat yourself to something you've been wanting for a while.

14. Give yourself Grace. Even when you feel like you don't deserve it. Give yourself Grace because you do deserve it.

15. Pray and write down your prayer requests. Then write down when your prayers are answered. Repeat.

16. Book the trip and get on the plane. On long stretches, such as summer weeks, spring break, etc. and your children are with their co-parent, book a trip or do something fun with friends.

17. Celebrate the Wins. Even if they seem small.

18. Designate a prayer space, big or small, have a space in your home just for you to pray and talk to God.

19. Create a vision board.

20. Make a Bucket List

Going through a divorce, separation of any kind, or facing grief can undoubtedly be some of the toughest challenges life can throw at you. But remember, tough times don't last, tough people do. Here are some encouraging words to help you navigate through your rooms of chaos in your lives.

1. **You are not alone.**
Find a support group for whatever you are going through. I guarantee there is already a space and support group for what you need. Reach out to your support system - friends, family, or professionals who can provide comfort and guidance.

2. **Change your perspective.**
If life feels chaotic right now, try to view it as a period of growth and transformation. Embrace this chance to rediscover yourself and rebuild your path.

3. **Know your worth.**
Your worth is not defined by your relationship status. You are strong, resilient, and capable of overcoming any obstacle that comes your way.

4. **Grieving is okay.**
It's okay to grieve the loss of your marriage and the life you once knew. Allow yourself to feel all the emotions, but don't let them consume you.

5. **Self-care is essential.**
Focus on self-care and nurturing your physical, emotional, and mental well-being. Make time for activities that bring you joy and peace.

6. *Give yourself time.*
Take things one day at a time. Healing is a journey, not a destination, and it's okay to progress at your own pace.

7. *Surround yourself with good vibes.*
Surround yourself with positivity and optimism. Listen to positive Podcasts, YouTube videos and positive affirmations. Believe that brighter days are ahead and have faith that you will emerge from this experience stronger and wiser than before.

8. *Trust in the process of life.*
Sometimes, the end of one chapter is just the beginning of a new chapter or new story. Trust God through the process.

9. *Practice forgiveness.*
Both for yourself and your ex-partner. Holding onto resentment only weighs you down and prevents you from moving forward. It's not worth it.

10. *Keep hope and love alive in your heart.*
Love may have disappointed you, but it has not abandoned you. There is still love out there waiting for you, whether it's in the form of new relationships, friendships, or self-love.

This path is an uncharted territory for me, one I've never traveled before and one that feels incredibly unfamiliar. I wrote this book with the intention of offering encouragement and support to other women and men who, like me, find themselves navigating the challenging journey of separation and divorce. It's tough to endure a separation. It's tough to go through a divorce. Yet, through the chaos and the struggles, there's solace in knowing that someone else is walking alongside you on this journey. My hope is that by sharing my experiences, I can reassure you that you are not alone, and that God is *always* in the room!

ABOUT THE AUTHOR
Latisha Richmond

About The Author
Author Latisha Richmond

Author Latisha Richmond is a mother, community leader, and successful sales professional who has faced challenges but used them to move from blessing to blessing. She resides in Burlington, North Carolina with her three boys.

Latisha holds a Bachelor of Arts in African American Studies from North Carolina State University. A persuasive communicator and tenacious negotiator, Latisha has held numerous sales and management positions. She is currently a New Home Sales Specialist, helping families to realize the *American Dream*.

When the chaos of her marriage reached a pivotal point, Latisha decided to step away from *"the societal marriage club"*. Throughout her journey through separation and on her road to divorce, Latisha takes you through all of the *Rooms* she has entered as she learned to accept and embrace her new life and co-parenting.

This book is unique in that it is not only about her journey managing life as a single mother, but it is her real-time account of her raw and transparent emotions and thoughts during that critical first transition year. Latisha highlights how she saw God, even through the chaos. Through her journey, Latisha realized that even though her marriage failed, she was not a failure!

IN A ROOM FULL OF CHAOS, WHERE DO YOU SEE GOD'S HAND?

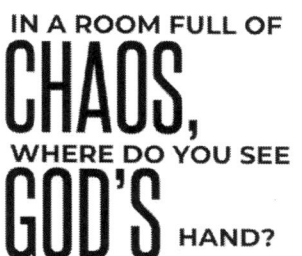

My Journey Through Separation & Divorce

LATISHA RICHMOND

While I may feel uncertain about this unfamiliar path that I find myself on, I take comfort in the knowledge that God has never let me down before, and I trust that He won't start now.

LATISHA RICHMOND

IN A ROOM FULL OF CHAOS, WHERE DO YOU SEE GOD'S HAND?

My Journey Through Separation & Divorce

shero publishing

Made in the USA
Columbia, SC
14 May 2025